The Secret Life of Elvis

Susan Doll, Ph.D.

Publications International, Ltd.

Susan Doll holds a Ph.D. in radio, television, and film studies from Northwestern University. An instructor of film studies at Oakton Community College and a writer of film and popular culture, she is a sought-after expert on the works and life of Elvis Presley. She has appeared on *The Joan Rivers Show* and National Public Radio to discuss Presley and other topics related to popular film. She is the author of numerous books on popular culture, notably *Elvis: A Tribute to His Life, The Films of Elvis Presley, Marilyn: Her Life and Legend, Elvis: Rock 'n' Roll Legend, Best of Elvis, Understanding Elvis, Elvis: Forever in the Groove, Elvis: American Idol,* and *Florida on Film.*

Additional Copyright Information:

Photo credits

Contents

Inside Elvis's Life and Career

Hundreds of books, biographies, and overviews have been written about Elvis Presley. How could there possibly be anything "secret" left to uncover? If the word "secret" is taken for its true meaning, there are actually many interesting aspects to the life and career of Elvis left to explore. Unfortunately, too many authors have used the word to titillate, sensationalize, or expose—sometimes with little respect or regard for their subject. Those looking for sordid stories, dirty laundry, or shocking facts will be disappointed in *The Secret Life of Elvis*.

"Secret" implies concealment, something that has been accidentally or purposefully hidden away. *The Secret Life of Elvis* offers stories, facts, and details that have been accidentally or purposefully cast aside, overlooked, understudied, or lost. Sometimes, a different perspective is considered on a story or detail that might seem insignificant on the surface, or a familiar story is found to be as much myth as biography. This book includes new insights, accurate details, and open secrets about Elvis Presley for all to share.

Elvis Presley was a major cultural figure of the 20th century. As such, secrets still swirl around him.

CHAPTER 1

Love Me Tender

The Presleys were a close-knit clan, dependent only on each other or a few relatives. As Elvis's father, Vernon, once said, "Though we had friends and relatives, including my parents, the three of us formed our own private world."

GLADYS LOVE SMITH PRESLEY

Elvis Presley's mother, Gladys Love Smith, was born in the flat farmland of Pontonoc County, Mississippi, not too far from Tupelo. Born into a large clan, Gladys shared what little the family had with seven brothers and sisters. Her father, who was a sharecropper and possibly a moonshiner, died when she was a teenager. She was forced to work to help support her family because her mother was sick with tuberculosis. When she was 21, she met handsome Vernon Presley, who was 17 years old. After a whirlwind two-month courtship, the couple married, but they lied about their ages

The close-knit nature of the Presley family is evident in this portrait of Vernon, Elvis, and Gladys in Tupelo.

on the marriage license. She said she was 19, and he claimed to be 21. On January 8, 1935, Gladys gave birth to Elvis Aron and his stillborn twin, Jesse Garon.

In an Elvis Presley story in which myth is too often taken as biography, Gladys is rendered as the devoted mother of the 20th-century's most famous entertainer as though her identity consisted only of that relationship. She is described as the fiercely overprotective mother who was unable to leave

her son in the care of anyone else for any length of time. She supposedly defended Elvis with a broom whenever older boys picked on him, and it is said that she walked him to and from school until he was an adolescent.

Certain biographers have used the memories and stories of eyewitnesses to assert that this behavior toward her son was reasonable; others use those same stories to claim this behavior was odd or peculiar. Still others point out that the stories themselves have been exaggerated through retelling. Most photos of Gladys show her in middle age. She is the melancholy, heavyset woman in a plain dress who stares out at the viewer with dark eyes made even darker by the circles beneath them.

Gladys's life before she was married is seldom explored and therefore a bit of a mystery.

But who was Gladys Love Smith Presley? What was she like as an individual in her own right? Did she have aspirations and dreams? Was she filled with satisfaction or regret?

As a young woman, Gladys was a tall, shapely, attractive lady with thick dark hair—a sharp contrast to her later photos. Though high-strung and nervous, she could also be bubbly and talkative. She had not been a good student in school, but she liked to interact with other boys and girls. As she grew older, Gladys continued to enjoy being with people, and her dark, sultry looks attracted the attention of country boys with nick-names such as Pid and Rex. She also socialized at the Church of God and Prophecy in Union Grove.

Despite a life of privation in the backwoods of the Deep South, Gladys had access to the 20th-century's two biggest contributions to mainstream culture—recorded music and the cinema.

Her neighbors down the road, the Reeds, bought a Victrola when she was teenager. The first records she heard were by Jimmie Rodgers, a country-western singer from Mississippi. The young country girl danced a wicked Charleston to his music with such energy and jubilation that old friends and neighbors remembered it long after she was dead. She had an innate sense of rhythm and a passion for music that inspired her to dance with bold abandon.

Vernon, Elvis, and Gladys Presley say good-bye on March 24, 1958, the day Elvis was inducted into the Army. Gladys looks distraught as Elvis prepares to leave for Fort Chaffee, Arkansas.

Gladys met handsome Vernon Presley after she moved to East Tupelo to work in a garment factory. She liked working in the factory, not because the work was interesting but because of her camaraderie with the other girls. During her early marriage, the vivacious young woman remained spunky, talkative, and eager to socialize, especially at the East Tupelo Assembly of God Church. Gladys, Vernon, and their friends and family loved to sing gospel music together, harmonizing on such standards as "The Old Rugged Cross."

As the years rolled by, economic and personal hardships took their toll, and the spunky young woman with a love of music

DR. WILLIAM ROBERT HUNT

DR. WILLIAM ROBERT Hunt delivered Elvis Aron Presley on January 8, 1935. He was 68 years old at the time, and the Presley twins were the 919th and 920th deliveries of his career.

Dr. Hunt, known as the "poor man's doctor," charged very low fees, even within a poor county in a Southern state during the Depression. He treated local mill workers, examined Army draftees and inductees, and took the welfare cases. His daughter, Sarah Hunt Potter, affectionately called him "an old country GP who poked along and never got ahead of himself."

Elvis was born in this modest house on Old Saltillo Road in East Tupelo. Elvis's grandfather, Jessie, raised it off the ground with field stones because of floods.

But he was much more than that. The delivery of Gladys Presley's twins had been a difficult one, and he sent her and her remaining twin to the hospital after the births. He was responsible for restoring her health and preserving the health of her infant. That this baby grew up to change the course of popular music did indeed make Dr. Hunt a significant figure.

Unfortunately, the good doctor did not live to see this occur. Dr. Hunt died in 1952—two years before Elvis recorded his first singles for Sun Studio.

and a gift for dancing faded away. Gladys remained warm-hearted, friendly, and gracious, but she grew into a nervous middle-aged woman, especially regarding Elvis. Responsibility and concern over the well-being of her only son consumed her.

Gladys is generally painted as a tragic figure because her life was hard by contemporary standards, and she died at the relatively young age of 46 in August 1958. Few offer a fuller portrait of the fun-loving country girl who danced the Charleston with wild abandon. While the two extremes are difficult to reconcile, Gladys will always be remembered for her depth of love for her son.

VERNON ELVIS PRESLEY

Vernon Presley was as sober and dour as Gladys was warm-hearted and outgoing. By the time he met pretty Gladys Smith, he had also experienced his share of hardships. He did not enjoy a close relationship with his father, the hard-drinking, hotheaded Jessie D. McClowell Presley, who kicked the unfortunate lad out of the house when he was only 15.

After Vernon and Gladys eloped on a whim, they had no place to live. Vernon dreaded telling his father, known as JD, about the marriage, because the elder Presley never had a kind word to say about this particular son.

The tightly-knit family of Vernon, Gladys, and Elvis found their lives turned upside down when Vernon was sent to Parchman Prison, a penal plantation in the delta region of Mississippi where the inmates worked the land in chain gangs. In November 1937, Vernon was indicted for forgery, along with Gladys's brother Travis Smith and

Gladys, Elvis, and Vernon make a somber group as they pose for a photo not too long before Vernon was sent to prison.

Lether Gable, and sentenced to three years in prison. The sentence seems harsh considering the crime: Vernon, Smith, and Gable had altered the figures on a check to Vernon from Orville Bean. Bean owned the land that Vernon had built his house on and frequently hired the young man as a laborer.

"PARCHMAN FARM BLUES"

About the same time that Vernon was incarcerated in Parchman, a bluesman named Booker T. Washington White may also have been a "guest" there. Nicknamed Bukka, White had been convicted of assault in 1937 but jumped bail and traveled to Chicago, where he recorded two songs. He was caught and returned to Parchman to serve a three-year sentence. After his release, he returned to Chicago to record 12 new songs, including his own composition, "Parchman Farm Blues."

Vernon sold Bean a hog for four dollars but felt the animal was worth a lot more and altered the figures on the check to compensate. The incident provides a snapshot moment of the Presleys' life in Tupelo. Elvis's poor childhood in the shotgun shack has become such a clichéd part of his life story that their abject poverty is lost beneath quaint stories of family togetherness and gospel singing at the Assembly of God Church. But this story is neither quaint nor colorful. Not only did Vernon's stint at Parchman result in the loss of their tiny home, but it also made it more difficult for him to find work.

After his release from prison, Vernon continued to work at a variety of jobs, moving his family from relative to relative, finding permanence in neither job nor home.

KINFOLK

Elvis not only felt a deep bond for his mother, but he was also close to his aunts, uncles, and cousins. After he became successful, he took care of many of them financially, just as some of them had taken care of Gladys and him during those early years in Tupelo.

One of the most colorful Presleys was Vernon's brother, Vester. As their names might suggest, Vernon and Vester, who were the oldest of J. D. Presley's clan, were very close while growing up. They did chores together, and they got into trouble together, including the time Vester lowered Vernon into the family's water well but was not strong enough to pull him up again. If he had let go of the rope to get help, the bucket would have slipped all the way into the water, and Vernon would have drowned. Vester had to hang on to the rope until his parents returned.

Vester and Vernon were constantly playing practical jokes on each other, a habit that carried over into adulthood. Like Vernon, Vester worked any job he could find to feed his family, including selling whiskey when Tupelo and Lee Counties were dry. A dry county meant that selling liquor there was illegal; several counties and states in the South were dry even after Prohibition ended.

Uncle Vester attends to Graceland's nativity display, December 1979.

A year after Vernon and his family moved to Memphis, Vester and his wife Clettes, who was Gladys's sister, followed. As the story goes—at least as it was always told by Vester—he showed a very young Elvis a few chords on the guitar. But Vester's greatest contribution to Elvis was his years as head gate guard at Graceland. From 1957 to his retirement in 1982, good-natured Vester manned the guardhouse by the famous Music Gates, and he became a favorite of fans. Charming, congenial, and always available for a photo, Vester was the perfect envoy for Elvis Presley and Graceland. Uncle Vester died on January 18, 1997.

Long after Elvis, Vernon, and Minnie Mae had died, Graceland still had a Presley in residence—Delta Mae Presley Biggs. One of Elvis's favorite relatives, Aunt Delta did not have children of her own, so she had doted on Elvis when he was a child, and Delta's husband, Pat Biggs, had always encouraged Elvis to pursue his goals and have faith in himself. Biggs died in 1966, and the following year, Elvis moved Aunt Delta to Memphis and put her on the payroll as a housekeeper and companion to her mother, Minnie Mae.

Delta was feisty and protective of Elvis. She was mistrustful of his buddy bodyguards who were collectively known as the Memphis Mafia. She suspected that many were hangers-on who were only after the gifts he frequently bestowed upon them. Hotheaded and argumentative, Delta was known to give several of Elvis's buddies a piece of her mind, whether they deserved it or not.

DOSHIA STEELE

One of the most interesting of Elvis's relatives in Tupelo was Doshia Steele, Mississippi's last widow of a Civil War veteran. Mrs. Steele was Jessie D. McClowell's sister, making her Elvis's great aunt. Elvis visited her at least once. He and his parents went to see her just before they moved to Memphis.

Graceland was opened to the public in June 1982. Fans eagerly tramped across the grounds and through the first floor, marveling at the furniture, keepsakes, photos, and decor. In what must have been an awkward arrangement, the second floor and kitchen area were off limits to tourists, because Aunt Delta continued to live at Graceland. Hundreds of tourists and fans visited Elvis's home each day, with Delta going about her daily routine just above them. Whether by choice or request from Elvis Presley Enterprises, Delta did not show herself. After she died in 1993, the kitchen was included on the Graceland tour, and in 1998, most of the upstairs was opened for public viewing.

Other relatives who worked for Elvis included maternal cousins Junior and Gene Smith, who traveled with him when he toured. Junior, who had been disabled during the Korean War, died tragically in 1961; Gene stayed with Elvis until the late 1960s, when he left after a disagreement. Elvis's uncles, Johnny and Travis Smith, worked as gate guards; cousins Billy and Bobby Smith served as personal aides. Patsy Presley, Elvis's first cousin and Vester and Clettes's daughter, began working as a secretary at Graceland in 1963. She befriended Priscilla and later married Elvis's chauffeur and valet, Marvin Gambill.

Many familiar stories, longtime myths, and cherished memories swirl around the Presley clan, both in Tupelo and Memphis. Whether exaggerated or truthful, most of them emphasize just how close the family was.

PRISCILLA BEAULIEU PRESLEY

Elvis met Priscilla Ann Beaulieu in 1959 while he was stationed in Germany during his stint in the Army. Much has been made of the fact that Priscilla was only 14 when the pair was introduced, but the young girl was mature for her age, and Elvis was mindful of the implications of the situation. Priscilla was photographed by the press at the airport when Elvis left the

Elvis and Priscilla relax in Palm Springs after their wedding.

LISA MARIE PRESLEY

AFTER HER FATHER'S DEATH in 1977, Elvis's only daughter was shielded from the public and the mainstream press by her mother, Priscilla Presley, who perhaps took a page out of Colonel Parker's book regarding the news media. As an adult, Lisa Marie appeared in the news upon occasion, but she never actively courted the press.

Currently, her relationship with her father's fans is connected to her role in his estate, which includes Graceland. She was scheduled to inherit the estate when she turned 25 in 1993. Instead, she formed a new trust, the Elvis Presley Trust, and retained the original three executors, including her mother. Five years later, her mother handed the trust over to Lisa Marie.

In 2003, Lisa Marie surprised the music industry and Elvis's fans by launching a career as a rock 'n' roll singer. Her debut album was titled *To Whom It May Concern,* and it reached number five on the Billboard 200, an albums chart. She released her second album,

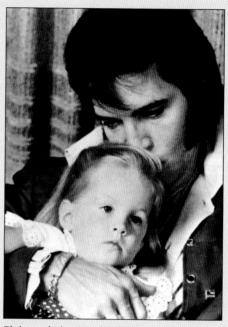

Elvis and Lisa Marie, December 1970.

Now What, in 2005, and it reached number nine on the Billboard 200. With her hard-rocking sound, she has carved out her own niche in contemporary music—no small feat considering the act she had to follow.

base in Germany to return to America, and some of those photos ended up in *Life* magazine. Beyond this, there was surprisingly little publicity about their relationship.

Priscilla visited Elvis at his home, Graceland, many times over the next couple of years, and Elvis began pressuring her parents to let her stay in Memphis. In 1962, he finally persuaded the Beaulieus to allow her to live with his father and stepmother, Vernon and Dee Presley, and attend school in Memphis. Gradually, Priscilla moved into Graceland while still underage. The press would have gone into a feeding frenzy if this information had leaked out, but while Priscilla was finishing high school, her private life remained private. More than likely, Colonel Tom Parker was responsible for keeping the news media at bay. He understood the press sharks and knew when and what to feed them. The dozens of stories about Elvis dating his leading ladies in Hollywood have become part of his image as a womanizer who chased the girls until they allowed him to catch them. Some of these stories were true, and some weren't, but they all created a smokescreen that protected Priscilla in Memphis.

Priscilla Presley poses at the Hyatt Hotel in Chicago for a Wella Balsam promotion, August 16, 1980.

On May 1, 1967, Elvis married Priscilla at the Aladdin Hotel in Las Vegas. The double-ring ceremony lasted only eight minutes and took place in the suite of one of the Colonel's associates. Only a few of Elvis's friends were allowed to witness the actual event, causing some dissension in the ranks of his buddy bodyguards. Afterward, there was a breakfast reception for 100 at the Aladdin, which was an event held primarily for the press. Elvis and Priscilla honeymooned in Palm Springs, California, and then split their time between Graceland and their new home in Beverly Hills.

On February 1, 1968, nine months to the day after Elvis and Priscilla were married, Lisa Marie Presley was born.

CHAPTER 2

Guitar Man

Elvis Presley constructed his music and his performance style out of rich, diverse musical traditions and influences—everything from Southern R&B to mainstream pop stylings. Who could have predicted that if someone mixed a dose of Arthur "Big Boy" Crudup with a portion of Bill Monroe, combined with a dash of Dean Martin, that it would come out as Elvis Presley?

ECAUSE HIS MUSIC was a unique combination of so many sources, he was always difficult to categorize and assess. This was true not only in the early days of rockabilly but also at the end of his career, when his sound evolved to incorporate a different blend of influences. Consequently, his musical career never followed

Elvis rocks the *Louisiana Hayride*.

the set path of previous performers, resulting in some unusual twists and turns that would have discouraged or ruined a lesser singer. It's a measure of the unique nature of his career that little known details, new insights, and profound conclusions can still be drawn from it.

A TRUCK DRIVER WHO RECORDED A SONG FOR HIS MOTHER

For decades, biographers claimed that Elvis Presley was a truck driver when he waltzed into the Memphis Recording Service to make a record for his mother. Those details solidified into a myth that helped turn his life into a comforting story of the American Dream—a humble truck driver who loved his family makes good as America's most famous entertainer. The truth is that Elvis was not a truck driver at the time, nor did he record the song for Gladys.

Elvis recorded "I'll Never Stand in Your Way" during his second visit to the Memphis Recording Service.

Elvis Presley entered Memphis Recording on a Saturday afternoon in late summer of 1953. The motto of the studio was "We Record Anything—Anywhere—Anytime." For four dollars, anyone could walk in off the street and record a two-sided acetate, and that was precisely what Elvis had come to do. Sam Phillips owned Memphis Recording and had been recording local artists for his label, Sun Records, for several years. Since Gladys's birthday was April 25, it is unlikely that Elvis stopped by to make a present for his mother.

Presley worked at the M. B. Parker Machinists' Shop at the time, a job he got after graduating from high school in June. Shortly after Elvis made his recording, Precision Tool hired him, along with his cousin Gene Smith, and the two of them worked on the assembly line making shells. While still at Precision, Elvis returned to Memphis Recording Service to make

BILL BURK: THE BEST MYTHBUSTER

BILL BURK KNEW Elvis Presley for almost 20 years, and as a reporter for the *Memphis Press-Scimitar*, he wrote more than 400 newspaper stories and columns about him. He met and made friends with most of Elvis's associates and family, which gave him access to stories and photos that other publications did not have.

In 1980, while still reporting for the newspaper, Burk helped fan clubs that wanted to coordinate events for Elvis Week. In 1986, while working in public relations, he launched *Elvis World*, a Memphis-based newsletter for fans all over the world. Readers have included former president Bill Clinton, the late Raisa Gorbachev, former USSR premier Boris Yeltsin, President Robert Mugabe of Zimbabwe, and Japanese prime minister Junichiro Koizumi.

In March 1960, Bill Burk interviews Sgt. Elvis Presley in Memphis after his discharge from the army.

Burk has written more than a dozen books on Elvis. He prides himself on his accurate information and in printing rare stories and photos from people who, in many cases, have never spoken to the news media. In this capacity, Burk has debunked many myths about Elvis, painstakingly researching and printing the true version of events to the benefit of fans and scholars.

---

another acetate in January 1954. This time he recorded "I'll Never Stand in Your Way" and "It Wouldn't Be the Same Without You."

In April 1954, Elvis got a job driving a parts truck for Crown Electric. He still held the job in June, when Sam Phillips called him to see if he was interested in recording a ballad for his Sun label. Though Elvis was working as a truck driver when he recorded his first commercial record, he did not hold that job when he made his two earlier acetates. No one knows exactly when the truck driver story began, but it was circulated in the press throughout 1956. A *Life* magazine article from April 1956 states that two years prior to his enormous success, he had been "a $35-a-week Memphis truck driver," a detail quickly picked up by the major papers.

In 1989, former Memphis reporter Bill Burk printed an accurate account of Presley's first recordings at Memphis Recording Service in *Elvis World,* disputing the old story that he was a truck driver when he was discovered. Recent biographies, including Peter Guralnik's definitive *Last Train to Memphis,* have incorporated Burk's research. Despite the findings of these well-respected authors, the myth continues to spin.

"ELVIS THE PELVIS"

Exactly where or from whom Elvis "borrowed" his legendary performing style for his live act has become another part of rock 'n' roll folklore. The truth is that his style, with its sensual hip movements and frenetic leg shaking, remains deceptively difficult to dissect. It was at once a hybrid of various influences as well as something unique to Elvis as an entertainer, something that differentiated him from other rockabilly or rock 'n' roll singers. Many biographers have claimed that Elvis's style was partly an influence from the flamboyant preaching style of Pentecostal ministers or the energetic performances of gospel singers Jake Hess and Jim Wetherington from the Statesmen. A witness to the musical developments on Beale Street from this era claims that Elvis got his wiggles from a black musician named Ukulele Ike, who played the blues at the Gray Mule on Beale. Such claims, however, result from speculation and a desire to dissect his music; they cannot be substantiated.

During the 1950s, Elvis was asked about his performing style ad nauseam in interviews across the country. Every disc

Throughout 1956, the mainstream press grew increasingly insulting in their descriptions of Elvis's sensual performing style, often comparing it to a freak show or a striptease.

jockey, local reporter, and teenager working for her high school newspaper asked him about it, and he patiently and sincerely answered them. He repeatedly explained that his movements were the result of feeling the rhythm of the music. He was simply expressing his enjoyment of the music as he sang. While often acknowledging his respect for other singers and performers, as well as his debt to them, he rarely—if ever—mentioned any influence on his live act.

In a recorded interview intended as a supplement to a magazine, Elvis offered a thoughtful account of his performing style. He believed that his R&B-influenced music inspired him to release his nervous energy while he sang. And, if that excited his audiences, then they were all taking "something out of our system and no one gets hurt." Besides, he wanted to give his audiences a good show and let them know that he really enjoyed the music he was singing. Uncovering the sources of both Elvis's musical sound and his performing style is important in understanding why his music was so revolutionary, but it is significant that Elvis integrated those influences into a stunning style that was ultimately all his own.

At the beginning of his career, when he was a regional performer down South, little mention was made of his shakes and shimmies. Publicity and promotional material from the early period simply described him as a hot young country singer with a crazy new sound that drove the young audiences wild. It was only after Elvis began performing for mainstream television audiences in 1956 that his unique performing style created controversy.

Reviewers for national magazines and major newspapers got into the habit of comparing his act to that of a stripper or burlesque dancer, implying that it was lewd or profane. As Tony Zoppie creatively reported in the *Dallas Morning News,* "...the gyrating pelvic motions are best described as a cross between an Apache war dance and a burlesque queen's old-fashioned bumps and grinds."

Elvis often took the high road when pressed about these accusations and denunciations, but secretly they must have bothered him because his anger and pain occasionally slipped out during recorded interviews. In the August 1956 interview in Lakeland, reporter Paul Wilder brought up a column by Herb Rau of the *Miami News* in which Rau rabidly criticized Elvis and his fans. Rau called the singer a "no talent performer" and "the biggest freak in show business," and he described the singer's act

WHAT'S IN A NAME?

During the 1950s, Elvis was billed as:

The Hillbilly Cat

The Atomic-Powered Singer

The Freshest, Newest Voice in Country Music

The Nation's Newest Singing Sensation

The King of Western Bop

The King

By 1958, when no moniker was necessary, the posters simply proclaimed: He's Coming!

as nothing but "pelvic gyrations" and "sex stimulations." Elvis countered by speculating that Rau was probably too old to have fun.

All the focus on his hips inspired some journalists to nickname the controversial singer "Elvis the Pelvis." The name infuriated Elvis, and he told reporter Paul Wilder and others that it was one of the most childish expressions he had ever heard from an adult. In retrospect, the controversy over his "gyrating hips" is often rendered in humorous tones or painted with a nostalgic brush. But the truth is that certain members of the press turned it into something quite ugly.

SECRETS OF THE ROAD: 1954–1958

Almost as soon as his career began, Elvis took to the road with the Blue Moon Boys to promote their records. By the time Elvis went into the army in 1958, he had played almost every state in the union. The early years on the road comprise one of the least documented aspects of his career but also one of the most interesting. The era begins when Elvis was young, optimistic, and completely unknown, allowing fans a glimpse of an unguarded man enjoying his good fortune as a promising new singer.

Elvis, Scotty Moore, and Bill Black began by playing any local venue that would have them, including the Overton Park Shell, local clubs—even the openings of shopping plazas. Soon they were playing farther from home, driving long distances for one or two shows here and there. Regular appearances on *Louisiana Hayride* brought enough recognition for the group to join talented country-western stars on packaged tours. Some of the tours were set

Elvis toured with country singer Bill Strength at least three times in 1955.

up by the *Hayride*, while others were organized by established promoters. These tours resulted in larger crowds, more venues, and the experience of working with an array of country music professionals ranging from established names to prominent newcomers. From 1954 to 1955, Elvis performed with country artists Bill Strength, Slim Whitman, Faron Young, Ferlin Huskey, Webb Pierce, the Wilburn Brothers, and Mother Maybelle and the Carter Sisters, plus up-and-coming stars such as Johnny Cash, Sonny James, and Charlie Feathers.

By 1956, when Elvis was exposed to a national audience, the crowds consisted mostly of teenage girls.

Elvis's music and performance style were decidedly different from traditional country, but he was a white singer from the South, and that automatically classified him as part of country music. Elvis always described himself as a spontaneous performer, naturally moving to the music, but the truth is that there was a measure of calculation in his performances. He exhibited an uncanny instinct for knowing what the fans wanted to see and hear. He teased them with a few hip and leg movements, they responded, and then he cut loose, singling out specific members of the audience to interact with. This phenomenon was reciprocal in nature, forming a strong bond between performer and audience.

Though notorious for attracting the affections of teenage girls during these years, the truth is that Elvis's look, music, and attitude also profoundly affected young men. He had a direct influence on aspiring singers such as Roy Orbison and Waylon

Jennings, who saw him perform when they were teenagers in Texas during the mid-1950s. Orbison, who remembered Elvis from the Big D Jamboree in Dallas, recalled, "His energy was incredible, his instinct was just amazing.... There was no reference point in culture to compare it." Jennings was 17 years old when he met Elvis and Scotty Moore backstage in Lubbock, and they made a strong impression on the teenager after they launched into "Tweedlee Dee" for him and his friends.

His music and performing style were so high-powered that other artists had difficulty following his act. By mid-1955, Elvis and the Blue Moon Boys were carefully positioned on the roster so as not to detract from the other performers. Faron Young, who became friends with Elvis, eventually refused to go on after him, because he knew that part of the audience was there to see this hot new singer and no one else. After Presley performed his three or four songs, they would either leave in droves or stand on their chairs and repeat, "Bring Elvis back," while other acts were on the stage. As Young told a promoter in Orlando, Florida, "I'm going on before Presley. That son of a bitch is *killing* the audience," which was show-business slang

WHAT KIND OF MUSIC IS THIS?

When Elvis began his career, the press did not use the phrases "rock 'n' roll" and "rockabilly" to describe music. Many had difficulty describing Elvis or his unique blend of musical genres. Some of their less-than-successful efforts include:

"rural rhythm" —*Memphis Press-Scimitar*

"His style is both country and R&B, and he can appeal to pop."
—*Billboard*

"the R&B idiom of negro field jazz"
—Robert Johnson, *Memphis Press-Scimitar*

"a boppish approach to hillbilly music" —*American Statesman*

"a hillbilly blues singer" —Charles Manos, *Detroit Free Press*

VEGAS FLOP

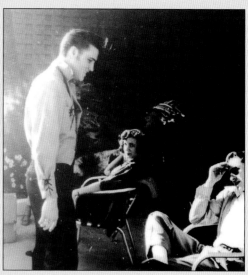

Elvis relaxes poolside at the New Frontier Hotel in Las Vegas in late April 1956.

*O*N APRIL 1956, the Colonel booked Elvis into a two-week engagement at the New Frontier Hotel in Las Vegas, a venture that turned out to be a disaster. Perhaps Parker should have known better than to book Elvis into a major engagement outside the South with an audience made up mostly of adults. After a few performances, Elvis was bumped to second billing in favor of a more typical Vegas entertainer, comedian Shecky Green. Stung by the rejection, Elvis would remember his failure in Las Vegas for many years. One good thing did emerge from the Vegas trip, however. Elvis was introduced to "Hound Dog" when he saw Freddie Bell and the Bellboys perform the song in the hotel lounge. "Hound Dog" became Elvis's signature song in 1956, ultimately bringing him as much controversy as fame.

for the way a singer excited a crowd to the point where no other entertainer could satisfy them.

After Elvis became a national sensation in 1956, he toured less often on a roster with established country stars. He was deliberately disassociated from country music by the Colonel and Steve Sholes of RCA while the press affiliated him with rock 'n' roll, hounding him about "those pelvic gyrations." Elvis released several hit records in 1956, but his act continued to run only about 20 minutes, because the audiences could be contained for only that length of time before crowd control became a problem.

OUT ON A LIMB IN 1968

After his performance on *The Frank Sinatra–Timex Special* on May 12, 1960, Elvis did not appear on television for seven years; after his benefit concert for the USS *Arizona* on March 25, 1961, he did not perform live for eight years. Instead, he turned his full attention to making films.

In 1968, Colonel Tom Parker announced that Elvis had signed with NBC-TV for a televised Christmas special sponsored exclusively by the Singer Company. The Colonel's idea was for Elvis to perform a selection of Christmas carols because his holiday albums had always sold so well. NBC, however, had hired a 23-year-old producer named Steve Binder who had a different vision. Binder wanted to prove that Elvis's music had been vital to the development of rock 'n' roll and that the singer was not a relic of the past. Binder and the Colonel fought bitterly over the television special, but the core of their differences lay in the perception of who Elvis really was.

Elvis joins the creative team behind *Singer Presents Elvis*. From left: producer Bones Howe, director Steve Binder, Elvis, and executive producer Bob Finkel.

If Binder was to succeed in turning his ideas for the special into reality, he had to encourage Elvis to go against the Colonel. Binder's secret weapon was to impress upon Elvis that his currency had deflated among younger audiences. He challenged Elvis to walk down Sunset Strip in Hollywood, where the special was being shot, to see if there would be any reaction from the young people who hung out there. Elvis had kept himself totally isolated from the public since he was discharged from the army, and he was reluctant to expose himself to an uncontrolled crowd. But Binder prevailed, and he, Elvis, and several members of the Memphis Mafia strolled nonchalantly down the Strip. No one noticed. Elvis tried subtly to attract attention to himself, but still no one indicated that they knew who he was. If anyone on Sunset Strip recognized Elvis, they didn't seem to care. Even though the crowd on the Strip was hardly a group of typical Americans, this experience convinced Elvis that he needed an edgy vehicle to put him on top again. In the battle of wills that ensued between Parker and Binder, Elvis sided with his young producer.

Elvis, which is now universally referred to as *The '68 Comeback Special,* aired on December 3, 1968. With a 32 rating and a 42 share, it was the highest-rated program for the week and the most-watched television special of 1968 by women viewers. Binder's executive producer, Bob Finkel, won a Peabody Award for his work on the show. Most important, it was a turning point in the career of Elvis: It was the moment when the real Elvis Presley roared back from the past to reclaim his crown as the King of Rock 'n' Roll.

SECRETS OF THE ROAD: 1970–1977

While Elvis's life on the road during the 1950s is relatively unknown, his concert tours of the 1970s are well documented by eyewitness accounts, newspaper stories, documentaries, and even home movies by fans.

A typical Presley concert of the 1970s was more like a series of rituals and ceremonies than a performance by a mere entertainer. Making his entrance to Richard Strauss's *Also sprach Zarathustra,* popularly known as the "Theme from *2001,*" Elvis charged into the spotlight as though propelled by some supernatural force. He incorporated karate kicks and tai chi arabesques into his act as well as other dramatic postures. Elvis also mocked his 1950s sex-symbol image by exaggerating the pelvic thrusts and sexual posturing of his old performing style, while making jokes about the "old days." More peculiar parts of his act included wiping the sweat from his brow and throwing the scarf or towel into the audience. This gesture became such a popular ritual that dozens of white towels were kept just offstage so that Elvis could throw them into the audience at frequent intervals. The most curious ritual of all was not performed by Elvis but by members of the audience. Each time Elvis played Las Vegas, the hotel stocked fresh undergarments in the restrooms because the women threw their underwear onto the stage while he was performing. Occasionally, they threw the keys to their hotel rooms.

One of the secrets of his concert successes during this decade was the illusion of intimacy that his onstage act conveyed. His rapport with his audiences was based on treating them like old friends or an extended family. Much interaction occurred onstage between Elvis and the audience members, such as the exchange of "gifts." Elvis threw towels and flowers into the audience; fans returned the gesture by throwing teddy bears, bouquets, and other mementos. Elvis kissed, hugged, and held hands with many of the women in the audience. They lined up just below the stage like a receiving line for royalty, waiting for the King to bless them with his touch. Audience members expected Elvis to sing specific songs and perform familiar moves; he always fulfilled those expectations.

Elvis sings "Love Me Tender" to the audience, mid-1970s. This song was the fans' cue to come down front to the stage to give flowers to Elvis, then kiss or hug him.

This type of interaction can be traced back to Elvis's early career, when audiences became hysterical at his gyrations and performing style. If his fans were unusually loyal and demonstrative throughout his career, this interactive aspect of his act—from the beginning of his career to the end—was partially responsible.

CHAPTER 3

Girls! Girls! Girls!

If Elvis could not leave the girls alone, then the reverse was also true. From fans to friends to femme fatales, women were an important part of the Elvis Presley story throughout his career, whether he was the dangerous rock 'n' roller, the handsome leading man, or the famous superstar.

LONG AFTER TALENT coordinator Horace Logan worked with Elvis Presley on the legendary radio program *Louisiana Hayride,* he recalled, "[Elvis] was absolutely crazy about girls. He loved them—both figuratively and literally.... During that period in his life, I never saw Elvis take an alcoholic drink.... I never saw him take so much as a puff from a regular cigarette, much less a marijuana cigarette. But he had an insatiable addiction to girls."

Elvis poses with showgirls during a visit to the Moulin Rouge nightclub in Munich, Germany.

TEENAGER IN LOVE: DIXIE, JUNE, AND ANITA

Much has been written about Elvis's teenage years in Memphis, some fact and some fiction. Part of the appeal of this phase of his life is that it allows a glimpse at an unspoiled young man who liked to bring home his best girl to meet his parents.

His first serious girlfriend was probably Dixie Locke—who had the perfect name for a nice Southern girl. The trajectory of their romance is like a walk back in time: She noticed Elvis at her church in 1953 when she was about 15; she spoke to him for the first time at a roller rink; they went to the movies on their first official date; she wore his class ring when they went steady; he escorted her to her high-school prom. Gladys Presley liked Dixie, and her family accepted Elvis, even though they found his mode of dress odd. Elvis and Dixie attended the Assembly of God Church, occasionally went to Reverend Brewster's African-American church to hear the music, and

Elvis leans against the green Lincoln, which Vernon bought for him when he was a high-school junior.

frequented the monthly All-Night Singings at Ellis Auditorium. The common denominator of these activities was gospel music, which both of them enjoyed immensely.

The young couple talked seriously about getting married, but Dixie soon had a rival for Elvis's affections—his career in the music industry. When Elvis recorded his first commercial single for Sun Records, the end of their relationship was inevitable. Her path toward a normal life, including marriage, family, and a home, was no longer his path.

After he began to tour to promote his Sun recordings in 1954 and early 1955, Dixie and Elvis drifted apart. Though he would call her while he was on the road, worried that she wouldn't be there for him when he returned, he was seeing other girls while he was touring. Dixie found it difficult to fit in with his new friends, whom she found coarse and wild. When he berated her for going out on the weekends with her girl-friends instead of staying at home, she knew he was being unreasonable. They broke up in the summer of 1955; Dixie married a year later, fulfilling her dream just as Elvis was fulfilling his.

Elvis hugs June Juanico, whom he dated in 1955 and 1956. June later wrote about her romance with Presley in *Elvis: In the Twilight of Memory.*

Elvis met June Juanico at a concert at Keesler Air Force Base in 1955 during her namesake month of June. Juanico had made eye contact with Elvis while he was performing, and during the intermission, she deliberately went to the ladies' room so she could walk by him. Elvis reached through the crowd of people surrounding him and grabbed her arm as she strolled by. He asked her to stay for his second set so that the two could go out afterward. June and Elvis hit it off and drove around Biloxi, Mississippi, for most of the night talking and getting acquainted. A year later, June visited him in Memphis, and they picked up where they had left off. June met Elvis's parents, feeling right at home with Gladys.

The next month, Elvis arrived in Biloxi to start a vacation, though his arrival was a surprise to June. They dated steadily for three weeks, which was the most prolonged span of time that they would spend together; the relationship was not on the same level as Elvis and Dixie's. If the press had not gotten wind of their romance, June Juanico might not be remembered today. Because the press rushed to print a story that the pair was engaged, June and Elvis jumped into a car and drove to New Orleans, where Elvis appeared on radio station WNOE to dispel the rumors in person. According to June, Elvis had promised Colonel Tom Parker that he would not do anything detrimental to his career for three years, including getting married, engaged, or even tied down with a girlfriend.

A month later while touring with Elvis in Florida, June answered a few questions from a reporter. She innocently admitted that she loved Elvis, while acknowledging that he was married to his career. Parker exploded with anger when he read the paper and demanded in front of the humiliated June that Elvis "do something about this." Later, Elvis did damage control by declaring to another reporter that he had 25 girls that he dated regularly, and June was just one of them. A few days later when June's mother was interviewed and spilled the beans about the seriousness of her daughter's relationship, the Colonel was livid once again. Elvis demanded Juanico call her mother and tell her to stay away from reporters. The incidents were telltale signs that when push came to shove, Elvis put the Colonel, his career, and even his fast-paced lifestyle first.

Like Dixie, June did not particularly care for the group of cousins and friends who toured with Elvis, mostly because he changed when he was around them. Also like Dixie, she did not fit into the show business side of his life, though the stakes were higher by the fall of 1956. By this time, Elvis's real-life girlfriends had to compete with Hollywood actors and actresses, slimy hangers-on, and a bicoastal schedule of appearances and movies. The continuing upward spiral of Elvis's career distracted him, and the phone calls to June became less and less frequent. When Elvis did not call her on Christmas Day, June learned it was because a Las Vegas showgirl was spending the holidays with him and his family. Brokenhearted, she began dating other boys. Shortly thereafter, she met someone who "swept me off my feet," and she married him.

The next small-town girl with whom Elvis got involved was Anita Wood, who was from Jackson, Tennessee, and who had show business ambitions herself. A beauty-contest winner, she was also a local Memphis television personality and disc jockey. She and Elvis began dating in 1957 after his buddy George Klein arranged an introduction. Though Elvis was no longer a teenager in love, Anita was just 19 when they began seriously dating. Anita was often photographed saying goodbye to Elvis as he left for Hollywood, a new tour, a recording session, or eventually the army in March 1958.

Anita was there for Elvis when his mother died in August 1958, consoling him as best she could. A Memphis newspaper leaked that Anita and Elvis would marry before he left for his tour of army duty in Germany the following month, but Anita fended off the report as mere rumor. Though Anita wrote regularly to Elvis in Germany, he was reluctant to have her visit him there. Shortly after Elvis returned home to Memphis, he and Anita resumed a relationship, but his situation had changed.

Elvis with Anita Wood, a local TV personality whom he dated off and on from 1957 to the early 1960s.

Just a few weeks before his army service was up, he had met 14-year-old Priscilla Beaulieu—the girl he would eventually mold into the woman of his dreams.

Anita wanted to get married and have a family, something she finally realized was never going to happen with Elvis Presley. In the summer of 1962, she broke off their relationship. Like Dixie Locke and June Juanico before her, Anita wisely gave up the most sought-after man in the world to pursue what she really wanted. Eventually, she married and had her own family.

MORE THAN JUST COSTARS

Early in his Hollywood career, Elvis developed a reputation for dating his costars while a movie was in production. Rumors about Elvis's crushes on actresses were always being repeated in fan magazines and elsewhere in the press. Much of what was said was obviously manufactured for its publicity value, but some of the rumors were undoubtedly true or came close to being true. To his credit, Colonel Parker kept information about Elvis's personal life to a minimum. He leaked just enough details about Elvis's Hollywood life to keep the news media away from Priscilla, who actually lived in Elvis's home, Graceland, although she and Elvis were not officially married.

Elvis kisses Ann-Margret, his love interest on- and off-screen during the shooting of *Viva Las Vegas* (1964).

Of all his relationships with his costars, Elvis's romance with Ann-Margret was probably the most serious. During the production of *Viva Las Vegas,* Elvis and the redheaded starlet set the publicity mill grinding when they began showing up together at restaurants and clubs around Las Vegas. They shared a mutual love for motorcycles and occasionally rode together, though they were warned to be careful because an accident involving either one of them would have delayed production on the movie.

The publicity surrounding the romance was a dream come true for the producers of *Viva Las Vegas,* but it must have been difficult for Priscilla. Secretly hidden from the public at Graceland, she undoubtedly saw the stories in Elvis's hometown newspaper, the *Memphis Press-Scimitar,* with headlines that blared "It Looks Like Romance for Elvis and Ann-Margret" and "Elvis Wins Love of Ann-Margret."

Although their romance did not work out for the long term, Elvis and Ann-Margret remained friends for the rest of his life. Elvis married Priscilla, and Ann-Margret married actor Roger Smith, but Elvis always sent Ann-Margret flowers in the shape of a guitar on the opening night of her Las Vegas engagements.

Elvis dated Tuesday Weld at the same time he was romancing Juliet Prowse, his costar from *G.I. Blues.*

Elvis also dated Tuesday Weld, his costar in *Wild in the Country.* Weld, who was barely 17 years old, was already a veteran of films and television as well as of the gossip columns. For good measure, Elvis also dated wardrobe girl Nancy Sharp about this time, whom he had met while filming *Flaming Star.* Other actresses whom Elvis dated during his career in Hollywood included Joan Blackman while working on *Kid Galahad,* Yvonne Craig while shooting *It Happened at the World's Fair,* Deborah Walley during the production of *Spinout,* and Mary Ann Mobley while working on *Girl Happy.*

A few actresses were notable for *not* dating Elvis during film production. Donna Douglas, costar of *Frankie and Johnny,* was a religious and spiritual person who impressed Elvis because she was so well read. He admired her intellect, and he was inspired by her example to read more, particularly books on religion and philosophy. Though Elvis tried desperately to get costar Shelley Fabares to go out with him during the production of *Girl Happy,* she was heavily involved with record producer Lou Adler and later married him. In lieu of a romantic relationship, Elvis and Fabares became friends. She costarred with him in two other movies, *Spinout* and *Clambake,* and Elvis later claimed that she was his favorite costar.

ELVIS AND THE BEAUTY QUEENS

After he and Priscilla separated, Elvis's next major relationship was with beauty queen Linda Thompson, who was Miss Tennessee at the time. The 22-year-old beauty had been invited by a mutual acquaintance to the Memphian Theater for one of Elvis's after-hours movie viewings. She and Elvis hit it off, and the next night, they enjoyed their first official date. Thompson left for a three-week vacation with her family, and while she was gone, Elvis dated another Memphis beauty queen, Cybill Shepherd, who had just appeared in *The Heartbreak Kid*.

Elvis was more smitten with Thompson, however, and invited her to his Las Vegas engagement in the summer of 1972. He caught her at just the right time in her life. After her reign as Miss Tennessee, she did not know whether to return to college, move to New York to pursue modeling, or try her luck in Los Angeles. She was ready to experience more of the world but was undecided which direction to take. The invitation to Elvis's world made the decision for her. She adapted to his lifestyle and centered her life around him. But instead of expanding her world, living with Elvis actually shrank it. They lived in an isolated hothouse atmosphere that was dependent on either his schedule or his whims.

In 1974, their relationship began to deteriorate as Elvis's drug use increased and his physical and spiritual health declined. In 1975, Linda left for Los Angeles to pursue her acting career, though she still accompanied Elvis on some of his tours. The following year, she left him for good, realizing that she couldn't make him happy or make him change his destructive lifestyle.

Memphis-born Ginger Alden was Elvis's last serious relationship. Longtime friend George Klein introduced the singer to the woman who would be his next girlfriend. Klein brought Alden and her older sister, Terry, to meet Elvis, though Klein thought that the singer might prefer Terry. Like Linda Thompson and Cybill Shepherd, the Alden sisters were beauty queens. Terry

A DATE WITH ELVIS AT THE MEMPHIAN

URING THE 1960s, Elvis began renting theaters and amusement parks after hours so that he could relax with some of his favorite activities but still have privacy. One venue that he rented regularly was the Memphian Theater on Cooper Street. The owner of the Memphian opened the theater after hours especially for Elvis, and he and his buddy bodyguards attended special film showings beginning at midnight. The bodyguards were allowed to bring outsiders, and sometimes the outsiders were allowed to bring friends as well. It was a way for Elvis and his friends to experience one of the most traditional dating activities—going to the movies—without the intrusion of the public. Elvis took many of his girlfriends to these after-hours affairs, and he met some of them there, including Linda Thompson.

The restored Memphian is now included as part of several Elvis Presley tours.

was the reigning Miss Tennessee, and 20-year-old Ginger was Miss Mid-South. Ginger became an official part of the entourage when she joined Elvis on tour in November 1976.

Ginger does not fit into the Elvis Presley myth and legend as nicely as Priscilla, who is still described as his true love, or Linda, who was well liked for her loyalty. According to some in his inner circle, Elvis asked Ginger to marry him because he was worn out, depressed, and lost in a haze of drug-induced disillusionment. Jeweler Lowell Hays claimed that Elvis had a diamond ring made for her from his own TCB ring (see sidebar on page 66) and proposed to her in January 1977. Whether he would have gone through with the marriage is still debated by those close to him. Alden might have been forgotten in the Elvis story if not for the fact that she discovered his body when he died on August 16, 1977.

CHAPTER 4

Change of Habit

Mary Reeves Davis, widow of singer Jim Reeves who appeared with Elvis on *Louisiana Hayride,* once mused, "Everybody has their own version of their relationship with and to Elvis. That's folklore. That's where folklore springs from. It's wonderful."

LVIS PRESLEY LEFT BEHIND no autobiography or even a definitive interview. Biographers and culture historians must rely on eyewitnesses to the times, newspaper accounts, musical experts, and even rumors to render a suitable portrait. Unmasking the *real* Elvis, the *true* Elvis, or the *secret* Elvis will always be one step removed from the original source. A glimpse at Elvis's everyday habits and personal tastes, however, as well as the press and public's response to them, offers a snapshot of the man offstage with all his idiosyncrasies, flaws, and complexities.

Elvis's personal tastes in regard to hair and clothing styles revealed a unique, expressive personality.

ELVIS'S HAIR

Outside of his music and performing style, the single most controversial aspect about Elvis Presley was not his Southern background, the Colonel, his night life, or even his love life—it was his hair! From the ducktail and sideburns at the beginning of his career to the blue-black locks of the 1970s, the amount of attention paid to his hair bordered on a national fixation.

Elvis's ducktail haircut is clearly visible in this photo taken in Las Vegas in May 1956.

In 1956, when rock 'n' roll was under fire across the country, the popular press not only skewered Elvis for his music and sensual performing style, but they also ridiculed him for anything that drifted from familiar mainstream tastes. He was maligned for his Southern accent, his lack of decorum, and his flashy clothes, but, most of all, they were severely critical of his long sideburns and ducktail haircut, which was so heavily laden with pomade that his blond hair looked black. Elvis's hairstyle was criticized because of its length, his use of pomade, and the fact that so many teenagers emulated it. His sideburns and ducktail haircut became a symbol of everything that made him different—and therefore threatening. To ridicule his hair was a defense against that threat.

Despite the criticisms, Elvis was proud of his hair, spending a lot of time grooming it for the right effect. While touring with Elvis in 1955, Jimmie Rodgers Snow looked on in amazement every morning as the nation's newest singing sensation combed his hair. Elvis used three different hair aids to get the effect he wanted. For the front, he used butch wax, a strong pomade designed for butch haircuts, and for the sides and back, he used two separate hair oils. He liked the sides to stay in place when he sang, but he wanted the front to fall in front of his face when he moved provocatively, because the effect made the girls scream.

Elvis's natural color was dark blond, though he made it look much darker. Shortly after finishing the film *Loving You*, he dyed his hair black, which became a permanent choice. Over the years, friends and biographers have speculated as to why Elvis preferred black hair: Some claim that he wanted his hair to match his mother's, whose own tresses were dyed black; others remember him saying that dark hair made his blue eyes stand out. More than likely, the color just appealed to him.

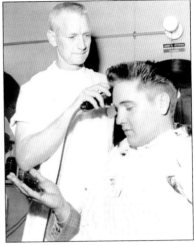

Elvis is inducted into the Army, March 24, 1958. The Colonel allowed reporters to record the day's events, including the shearing of his famous ducktail haircut.

From 1956 to 1958, the constant focus on his hair made it part of his image as the rebellious rock 'n' roller and potent sex symbol. No wonder when the Army shaved off his hair in March 1958, the press was there to photograph every chunk of hair that fell from his head. In 1960, when he resumed his career after his stint in the Army, the Colonel, producer Hal Wallis, and his Hollywood agent decided that a more mature, well-groomed image was needed for Elvis to steer him away from controversy and to gain acceptance by the mainstream audience. Appropriately, his ducktail haircut never grew back.

"THE MOST ICONIC HAIRSTYLE"

Thirty years after his death, Elvis's hair is still distinctive. In a 2006 British poll taken by *Argos*, Presley's hair was voted "the Most Iconic Hairstyle Ever." The Beatles' famous mop tops were voted #4.

By the end of the 1960s, Elvis's well-groomed leading-man style looked old-fashioned. *The '68 Comeback Special* not only reintroduced Elvis as vital musical force but also showed him with a hipper hairstyle and longer sideburns. As the 1970s progressed, this hairstyle and the accompanying mutton-chop sideburns grew longer. Though little was made of it at the time, after his death, his hair and sideburns once again became the source of attention. Along with the white jumpsuits, the distinctive hairstyle made it easy for even the worst impersonator to offer a recognizable impression of Elvis Presley.

CLOTHES MAKE THE MAN

Many of the candid photos of Elvis onstage or with fans from the 1950s are in black and white. If they were in color, they would reveal another reason why the press found Presley so

strange. More than likely, he was wearing a kelly green jacket with bright blue pants, or a red satin shirt with a loud tie, or white buck shoes with red heels, or some variation of pink and black.

Elvis's taste in clothes are part of his myth, and every fan knows that during his early career, he purchased many of them at Lansky Bros. on Beale Street in Memphis. Owned and operated by Bernard and Guy Lansky, the store began as an Army surplus store after World War II but evolved into a clothing store that catered to African-American R&B artists and white rockabilly singers. Most of the outrageous attire that surprised the press in the mid-1950s undoubtedly came from Lansky's.

Bernard Lansky fits his most famous client in Lansky's Clothing Emporium at 126 Beale Street.

Elvis bought at least one of his high-school prom suits at Lansky's, and Bernard was the one who fitted him for it. The circle was closed in 1977 when Lansky's provided the suit that Elvis was buried in. Bernard made the white burial suit especially for him, accented by a white tie. In a simple but touching comment, the old clothier remarked, "I put his first suit on him, and I put his last suit on him."

One suit that Elvis did not purchase at Lansky's was the legendary gold jacket and slacks woven from spun gold thread, with a matching string tie and white ruffled shirt. Elvis asked the famed Hollywood clothing designer Nudie Cohen to create this special suit for him for his 1957 tour across the northern United States and parts of Canada. Critics and journalists responded to Elvis in his gold suit like a bull to a red flag. Along each leg of the tour, newspapers never failed to mention the legendary gold tuxedo. Though other entertainers, particularly Liberace, could wear outrageous costumes without criticism, Elvis was always ridiculed or criticized.

A taste for sartorial splendor also marked Elvis's image during the 1970s, when he returned to the stage to perform before live audiences. The jumpsuits, which were designed by Bill Belew, were an original touch to his act that became iconic of this era, though they have since been appropriated by impersonators and turned into a ridiculous stereotype of Elvis. Belew designed some of Elvis's offstage wardrobe, which often included accents like high collars, open necks, multicolored scarfs, and colorful shirts. Elvis liked to accessorize with canes, capes, jewelry, and oversize jeweled sunglasses.

LANSKY'S RECYCLED

The building that used to house Lansky's on Beale Street has been used by many organizations and businesses over the years, including the Center for Southern Folklore and EP's Memphis Restaurant. In 2006, Memphis restauranteur Jimmy Ishii opened the EP Delta Kitchen and Bar in Lansky's former location.

Elvis's personal taste in clothing and accessories was never ordinary.

THE BLACK LEATHER SUIT

FOR ONE SEGMENT of *The '68 Comeback Special*, Scotty Moore and D. J. Fontana reunited with Elvis onstage for an informal jam session. The black leather ensemble that he wore in this segment has become one of Elvis's most famous costumes. Designed by Bill Belew, the costume has become synonymous with Elvis's creative comeback in the late 1960s. Like the new arrangements of his songs, the black leather outfit recalled the past but did not duplicate it. The comeback special aired at the close of 1968, when flower children held love-ins and wore paisley and posies. In the midst of the Age of Aquarius, a drop-dead handsome Elvis Presley strolled onstage in black leather, a guitar cocked on his hip, and reminded us that rock 'n' roll was not about peace and harmony—it was about sexuality and rebellion.

Elvis in his leather suit reminds his fans of a younger Elvis.

Just as he had always expressed himself with free abandon in his bold, innovative music, he also expressed himself through his clothing. Like his music, his look was an affirmation of his originality, his desire to stand out from the crowd, and his effect on mainstream America, which was to shake the nation out of its complacency. As Elvis himself said about clothes: "They say things about you that you can't, sometimes."

THE GUNS

Elvis collected guns and other kinds of weapons. He was especially fond of a huge .44 magnum, a little derringer similar to those carried by 19th-century riverboat gamblers, a turquoise-handled Colt .45, and a pearl-handled undercover .38. Elvis also lavished expensive guns on his buddy bodyguards, also known as the members of the Memphis Mafia.

During the 1970s, Elvis carried a gun with him at all times because he was concerned for his safety. After he began performing again in Las Vegas, Elvis received many death and kidnapping threats. He believed that assassins were almost always seeking glory or media attention when they tried to kill a famous person and that they were so eager for fame that they were willing to chance death or living out their lives in prison to attain recognition. In 1971, while Elvis was performing in Las Vegas, an anonymous caller got through to his hotel room and warned him that there would be an assassination attempt during that evening's performance. Later that day, Elvis received a menu from the International Hotel with his picture on the front. The picture had been defaced, and a handgun had been drawn near Elvis's heart. A message included with the menu read, "Guess who, and where?" The hotel management told him he did not have to go on, but Elvis stuck a Derringer into his boot and a .45 into his belt, and did the show anyway.

Elvis shows off part of his gun collection, much of which is currently on display in the Trophy Room at Graceland.

During another incident in Las Vegas in 1973, four drunks suddenly bolted onstage during Elvis's midnight show. Elvis's close friend and bodyguard Red West subdued one of the men, and three members of the Memphis Mafia, Vernon Presley, and one of the Colonel's assistants scuffled with two others and eventually dragged them offstage. Elvis knocked the fourth man off the stage himself and sent him hurtling into the crowd. Then Elvis apologized to the audience, telling them he was sorry; that is, he was sorry he didn't break the man's neck. This statement brought down the house; there was a seven-minute standing ovation from the crowd.

THE BADGES

Because Elvis was infatuated with law enforcement, he collected police badges wherever he went. Elvis asked the sheriff of Shelby County, Tennessee, to give him, his father, his doctor, and most members of the Memphis Mafia deputy's badges. Elvis also had a badge from the Palm Springs Police Department, and he had close friends who were members of the Los Angeles Police Department and the Denver Police. The *pièce de résistance* of his collection was the federal agent's badge, which a reluctant John Finlator gave to him in Washington, D.C.

President Richard Nixon presented this Federal Narcotics Bureau badge to Elvis in December 1970.

Considering that Elvis once had an image as a rebel who opposed authority and actually was arrested in 1956 for fighting with a gas station attendant, it's ironic that he came to have so much respect and admiration for law enforcement officials.

FOOD

Because of his wealth and celebrity status, Elvis could indulge himself to excess, but exactly how much he overindulged his bad habits has been overstated. The exaggerations of his kingly excesses have become part of his legend, including those involving his eating habits and choice of foods.

Elvis was a lifelong fan of junk food and Southern-style cooking. As early as 1955, when he was still considered an up-and-coming country-western singer, articles about the hot, young singer often mentioned that he liked to down several cheeseburgers in one sitting. An article in *Esquire* magazine in the late 1960s took a sarcastic but lighthearted tone when describing Elvis's favorite snack of peanut butter and mashed banana sandwiches washed down with several Pepsis. After

Elvis's death, this kind of report on his eating habits took on a sinister connotation in some of the biographies. Many used these stories to "prove" that Elvis was losing control as his career progressed and that his eating habits and weight problems foreshadowed his drug abuse. These attempts at armchair psychology don't take into account the fact that Elvis ate the same way all his life.

Most of Elvis's favorite foods were typical Southern dishes, which often include heavily fried meats. Biographers who were not familiar with Southern cooking felt that Elvis's eating habits were peculiar, although many people in the South enjoy the same foods that Elvis liked to eat.

At the end of his life, Elvis's problems with his weight became apparent.

While Elvis had many unhealthy eating habits and gained a great deal of weight, the stories about what he ate are often widely exaggerated. It's as though Elvis's larger-than-life image, particularly during the last phase of his career, required tall tales of eating feats to support his legendary status.

CHARITY

Tales about Elvis's generosity to complete strangers have become part of his legend. Once, while he was buying a couple of El Dorados for members of his entourage, Elvis noticed a young couple who were wandering around the dealer's lot, trying to find a car that they could afford. Elvis told them to pick any car they wanted, then he wrote out a check and left the salesman to do the paperwork. Another time, he gave away seven Cadillacs and Lincolns to people in Colorado.

Elvis was also generous in less flamboyant ways. On the flight to Washington, D.C., to see the president, Elvis noticed a soldier who was returning home for the Christmas holidays. Knowing firsthand how little money people in the service are paid, Elvis told his traveling companions to give the soldier all of their cash. They gave him about $500, which meant that Elvis and his friends had to rely on their credit cards to pay for the rest of their trip. Another time, Elvis gave $500 to a blind man who was selling pencils. When he read in the paper about a poverty-stricken black woman in dire need of a wheelchair, Elvis bought her a motorized chair and delivered it himself. Many times, when he saw a news report about a police officer who had been killed, Elvis called the television station to get the name of the officer's widow so that he could send her money.

Elvis used his status as an entertainer for good causes, and some of his most famous concerts were benefits. On September 26, 1956, he returned to his hometown of Tupelo to give two shows at the city's annual Mississippi-Alabama Fair and Dairy Show. The event was known as the Homecoming, and Mayor James L. Ballard gave him the key to the city. Elvis earned about $20,000 that day, which he promptly handed over to Mayor Ballard to purchase his birthplace and the surrounding land as a park for the city.

In 1961, he performed live in concert only twice, both times for charity. On February 25, he gave a concert in Memphis, and the proceeds were distributed to 38 charities. On March 25, he appeared at a benefit in Honolulu to raise money for the U.S.S. *Arizona.* Just over a year later, the Memorial for the U.S.S. *Arizona* was dedicated.

In 1973, Elvis returned to Hawaii for another benefit performance, which most fans remember as the *Aloha From Hawaii Via Satellite* concert. Broadcast around the world, the concert is famous because it was beamed to several countries via the Intelstat IV communications satellite. Few realize that the concert was designed to raise money for the Kui Lee Cancer Fund. Lee, best known for writing the song "I'll Remember You," had been a Hawaiian entertainer who died of cancer in 1966. Elvis reportedly raised $75,000 for the fund.

In May 1975, Elvis raised over $100,000 for the victims of a tornado that had ravished his home state of Mississippi. He also donated to organized charities, though he never wanted any publicity for it. Every Christmas, Elvis and Vernon donated $1,000 checks to at least 100 Memphis charities, including every organization from the Boys Town of Memphis to the Jewish Community Center to the Epilepsy Foundation.

In 1971, Elvis was named by the U.S. Jaycees as one of the Ten Outstanding Young Men of America. Each year the Jaycees selected ten men who represented "the young ideals that are vital to the growth of America." The group recognized Elvis as the greatest entertainer of his time, but they also selected him because of his philanthropy. As the official proclamation declared, "Throughout his career Elvis has been one of the most civic-minded residents of Memphis, Tennessee.... Unlike many entertainers, he has intentionally concealed many acts of philanthropy."

At the ceremony for the Ten Outstanding Young Men of America, Elvis stands next to fellow honoree Thomas Atkins.

The Jaycees award consists of a pair of silver hands, and it is currently on display at Graceland. Visitors are apt to notice that the award has many scratches and scuff marks, looking as though it has seen better days. The reason is because Elvis carried the statue on every tour and on every vacation. It was always placed next to his bed within his reach.

Few entertainers could match Elvis Presley for his generosity, which seems a more fitting reflection of "the secret Elvis" than stories of his excesses and flaws.

CHAPTER 5

Flaming Star

"A Presley picture is the only sure thing in Hollywood."

—PRODUCER HAL WALLIS

AS A TEENAGER IN MEMPHIS, Elvis went to the movies with friends Farley Guy, Paul Dougher, and Buzzy Forbess, most of whom lived in Lauderdale Courts, the federal housing project that Elvis called home for several years. Elvis was a lifelong fan of the movies, long before he himself was a star. As a boy, he preferred westerns and the Tarzan series with Johnny Weissmuller, and as he grew older, he became a fan of Tony Curtis. Curtis had gained attention in *City Across the River,* a gritty urban drama about life in the Brooklyn slums. Elvis caught Curtis in this seminal film either at the Suzores #1 on Main Street or the Rialto on Jackson, the two theaters he regularly attended with his friends. The boys also liked Victor Mature in *Samson and Delilah.*

Elvis enjoyed one of his few
serious roles in *Flaming Star,*
directed by the great Don Siegel.

Though this biblical epic may seem an odd choice for a group of teenage boys from the Deep South, Mature's masculine presence made an indelible impression.

Even after he broke into Hollywood, Elvis remained a film fan. As an adult, he rented the Memphian and the Malco for private showings for him, his entourage, and invited guests. Their personal screenings began late in the evening and continued through the night, one film after another until about 6:00 A.M. As Presley insider Alan Fortas once said, "Believe me, he was a very avid movie fan." Hal Kanter, the writer-director of *Loving You*, echoed this sentiment.

The Malco Theater sign looms behind Elvis in this August 1956 photo. Elvis was not yet a star.

A consideration of his favorite films offers a bit of insight into his attitude toward his own film career. Many claim that his favorite film was *Patton*, the story of the eccentric and notorious WWII general. Other favorites included the dramas *To Kill a Mockingbird*, *The Godfather*, *The Wild Bunch*, *A Streetcar Named Desire*, *The Man with the Golden Arm*, and *One Flew Over the Cuckoo's Nest*. Most of these films have in common a strong, career-changing performance by a powerful, talented actor in the role of the protagonist. In addition, Peter Sellers's tour de force in multiple roles in *Dr. Strangelove* made this film one of Elvis's all-time favorites and Sellers one of his favorite comic actors.

Like all film buffs, Elvis had his personal favorites among less-acclaimed fare. He was a major fan of Monty Python movies. He also liked the colorful blaxploitation films, particularly *Shaft* and *Superfly*, and thought the crime drama *Across 110th Street* was underrated. Elvis's tastes in films seemed to lean toward serious drama, edgy comedy or satire, and dark action fare. Given his personal preferences, it is clear why he held such disdain for his own lighthearted musical comedies. As Farley Guy recalled about the old movie-going days in Memphis, "None of us cared much for the musicals."

COULD ELVIS HAVE BEEN A DRAMATIC ACTOR?

Elvis was eager to be a bona fide actor, which is evident from his comments to the press after he signed a contract with producer Hal Wallis. In an interview with Bea Ramirez on April 19, 1958, for the *Waco News Tribune,* he told her he wasn't

going to sing in his first film, which he thought would star Katharine Hepburn and Burt Lancaster. The film he was talking about was *The Rainmaker,* based on a prominent play by N. Richard Nash. Though Elvis had made a screen test for Wallis in which he played a part from *The Rainmaker,* he did not end up in the final film. The part he had read for his screen test, which he assumed he would get, eventually went to Earl Holliman. Instead, Wallis loaned Elvis

This lobby card shows Elvis singing in *Love Me Tender,* revealing how his image as a rock 'n' roller overshadowed his acting career.

to 20th Century Fox to be in the Civil War western *The Reno Brothers,* later retitled *Love Me Tender* after the theme song Elvis sang in the film. The decision to alter the film's title to accommodate Elvis's song foreshadowed his entire career, in which any potential he held as a dramatic actor was undercut by his identity as a recording star. Wallis, Colonel Tom Parker, and Abe Lastfogel of the William Morris Agency preferred Elvis to star in vehicles tailored around his existing image as a recording artist rather than to allow him to stretch as an actor.

ELVIS'S BEST COSTARS

ELVIS WORKED WITH some of the best actors in Hollywood, past and present. Some were movie stars, some starlets, some character actors, and some veterans from another era, but all added depth and professionalism to the performances in the films.

Richard Egan in *Love Me Tender*

Walter Matthau and Carolyn Jones in *King Creole*

Juliet Prowse in *G.I. Blues*

Dolores Del Rio and John McIntire in *Flaming Star*

Angela Lansbury in *Blue Hawaii*

Gig Young in *Kid Galahad*

Tuesday Weld in *Wild in the Country*

In *King Creole* (1958), Walter Matthau plays tough guy Maxie Fields and Elvis plays rebellious teenager Danny Foster.

Ann-Margret in *Viva Las Vegas*

Barbara Stanwyck in *Roustabout*

Joan Blondell in *Stay Away, Joe*

Sheree North in *The Trouble with Girls*

Mary Tyler Moore in *Change of Habit*

From Elvis's perspective, this strategy shattered his dream of becoming a dramatic actor, as pop singers Bing Crosby or Frank Sinatra had done. Crosby and Sinatra had been the biggest singers of their respective eras, but both had branched out into legitimate acting, and both won Academy Awards. Elvis had planned on modeling his career after theirs, but his management team urged him to continue with a less risky course.

When the story of Elvis's film career is recounted in biographies, Parker and Wallis's strategy is criticized for destroying Presley's potential as an actor and his creativity as an innovative rock 'n' roller. While there is no doubt that the Colonel drove Elvis's Hollywood career to a dead end by the mid-1960s, the road there was not a simple or straight one. If Elvis had continued to make serious movies, such as *Flaming Star* and *Wild in the Country,* which were less successful at the box office than his musicals, there is no guarantee he would have enjoyed the career he envisioned. Throughout the history of Hollywood, scores of performers from other arenas of entertainment experienced only limited success in motion pictures, while some completely failed. During Presley's era, several pop stars embarked on Hollywood careers but ended up with less success than Elvis, even after they attempted serious roles. Why would Elvis have succeeded as a serious actor when singers Fabian, Tommy Sands, and Frankie Avalon had not?

Tuesday Weld was as talented as she was charismatic. In *Wild in the Country,* she stole most of her scenes—even those with Elvis.

Given his image as a notorious rock 'n' roller, some have assumed that Elvis would have followed in the rebel footsteps of James Dean and Marlon Brando if given the chance in a real role. Both Dean and Brando, however, had studied the Method approach to acting at the prestigious Actors Studio in New York City, while Elvis was untrained. During Elvis's heyday in Hollywood, the new wave of legitimate actors who invaded the film industry had studied acting as a craft either in college or in New York. How far Elvis's charisma and natural ability could have taken him in serious drama is open to debate.

ELVIS PAYS FOR *BECKET*

Looking at Elvis's career from Wallis's perspective, it becomes clear that he had a specific strategy for the Presley pictures that he produced, and his plans did not entail Elvis becoming a serious actor. Wallis had been in the film industry since 1923, and because he knew the value of star charisma to draw an audience, he used Elvis's image and magnetism to lure his fans to his movies. From *Loving You* to *G.I. Blues* to *Easy Come, Easy Go* (the last Wallis-produced Presley musical), the savvy producer was interested in making vehicles tailored to Elvis's image, because they always made a profit. Wallis then put up the potential profits guaranteed by an Elvis musical as collateral to finance more prestigious films. For example, he used the potential profits of *Roustabout* as a guarantee for the backers who invested in his production of *Becket*, which won an Academy Award for best adapted screenplay. Some members of his inner circle claimed that Elvis complained bitterly but privately about *Becket*, feeling that Wallis had used him.

Elvis and his famous costar Barbara Stanwyck on the set of *Roustabout* (1964).

The truth is that no one on Elvis's management team was interested in his desire to be a serious actor, because it made little sense by Hollywood standards. His Hollywood agent, Abe Lastfogel, was dedicated to maintaining Elvis's stardom, which meant playing to his existing star image as a pop singer; Wallis needed the profits from the films to produce his more artistic films; and the Colonel wanted to continue to rake in the profits for himself and his client.

Even after Wallis saw the writing on the wall and realized that his Presley series was running its course, Elvis's musicals continued to make money for other producers and production companies. In 1965, Allied Artists released *Tickle Me*, starring Elvis, Julie Adams, and Pam Merritt, which became the third-highest-grossing film in the history of the company. Allied had been in financial difficulty prior to signing with Parker for a Presley vehicle, but *Tickle Me* pulled them back from the brink of bankruptcy.

Ultimately, there is more than one way to consider Elvis's film career. From Elvis's perspective, he had been coerced into making a genre of film he did not like personally, and his dreams of being a serious actor had been thwarted. Small wonder that he ridiculed his film career throughout the rest of his life. Biographers tend to depict his Hollywood career in similar terms, blaming the films for taming his rebel image and sympathizing with the waste of his acting talents. From the perspective of his management team, however, his films were quite successful. And when the Presley vehicles stopped being lucrative for most of the parties involved, the Colonel let the contracts run their course, and Elvis stopped making movies.

The only perspective that remains today is that of the fans. Almost 40 years after he made *Change of Habit,* his cinematic swan song, fans still enjoy his movies, which for the most part are well-crafted reminders of another time and place. Rather than bemoaning Elvis's squandered talent and missed opportunities, it is more fruitful to accept what he offered.

However tragic Elvis's sojourn in Hollywood was on a personal level, his movies and sound track recordings not only made him one of the highest paid actors during the mid-1960s but also made him a true international superstar.

THE CAREER OF RED WEST

In 1955, Elvis's former classmate, Red West, joined him on the road as an extra driver and bodyguard. After shows, overzealous fans sometimes accosted Elvis, and Red was on hand to help him get into the car safely. Even more dangerous were the jealous boyfriends of frenzied females who had been driven to hysterics by Elvis's performance. The jilted young men were often

Bodyguard Red West, who worked for Elvis from 1955 to 1976, later became a successful character actor.

SMALL PARTS FOR BIG ACTORS

SOME OF THE FUN in watching Elvis's films is to recognize interesting actors in bit roles.

• **Charles Bronson,** a major action star of the 1970s, costarred as Lew Nyack in *Kid Galahad.* Also, a young **Ed Asner,** who played Lou Grant in two highly successful television series, made the most of a small role in this film.

• **Teri Garr,** the girl-next-door in several famous films of the 1980s, can claim the crown for appearing the most in bit parts in Elvis films. Look fast and you can see her as a dancer in *Viva Las Vegas, Roustabout,* and *Clambake,* and as an extra in *Kissin' Cousins* and *Fun in Acapulco.*

• **Raquel Welch** showed up in *Roustabout* as a college girl.

• **Dan Haggerty,** who enjoyed fame as the title character in TV's *Grizzly Adams,* played Charlie in *Girl Happy.*

• **Christina Crawford,** Joan Crawford's daughter and author of *Mommie Dearest,* played Monica George in *Wild in the Country.*

Charles Bronson became a major action star a few years after his role in *Kid Galahad.*

• **Michael Murphy,** one of Woody Allen's key actors during the 1970s and the star of the innovative TV miniseries *Tanner '88,* made his second screen appearance as Morley in *Double Trouble.*

• **Dabney Coleman,** everyone's favorite oily villain in such films as *9 to 5,* played Harrison Wilby in *The Trouble with Girls.*

• **Jane Elliot,** who has played Tracy Quartermaine on *General Hospital* for two decades, got her big break as Sister Barbara Bennett in *Change of Habit.*

looking for a fight, though they tended to back down when they realized they were no match for Red West.

After Elvis was discharged from the army, West rejoined the Presley entourage as a bodyguard, but he carved out a second career for himself as a stuntman and bit player in Hollywood. Most fans recognize West in walk-ons or fight scenes in *Flaming*

Star, Blue Hawaii, Follow That Dream, Roustabout, Tickle Me, Clambake, and many more Presley vehicles.

In 1976, Vernon Presley fired West, prompting West to co-write the infamous bodyguard biography *Elvis: What Happened?,* which was published just a few weeks before Elvis's death. Most fans know Red West only from this notorious episode at the end of Elvis's life, but West's own acting career—one

Former bodyguards Dave Hebler, Red West, and Sonny West read about their infamous book in the tabloids.

outside the confines of the Elvis myth—was just beginning to take off in earnest. In 1977, West landed the role of Sgt. Andy Micklin in Robert Conrad's series *Baa Baa Black Sheep.* Throughout the 1980s and early 1990s, he acted in episodic television, appearing on a variety of popular television dramas. In the mid-1990s, his career evolved once again when he worked as a character actor in a number of films by prominent directors, including Oliver Stone's *Natural Born Killers,* Francis Coppola's *The Rainmaker,* and Robert Altman's *Cookie's Fortune.*

Unlike Elvis, West studied his craft professionally, taking lessons from character actor Jeff Corey, who taught Stanislavskian techniques at his Professional Actors Workshop in Los Angeles. The fruit of West's experience at Corey's workshop is evident in his role in the 1997 film *The Rainmaker,* a drama based on John Grisham's novel and one of Francis Coppola's last directorial efforts. (This movie should not be confused with the play by N. Richard Nash.)

Though never a famous film or television star, West continues to enjoy a successful career as a character actor in Hollywood dramas (*Glory Road*) and in respected independent productions (*40 Shades of Blue*). Ironically, West has experienced the kind of serious acting career that Elvis had always wanted.

CHAPTER 6

Stand by Me

Like all kings, Elvis had his court. The entertainment press called this group of close friends, business associates, and employees "the Memphis Mafia."

THEY NOT ONLY WORKED for Elvis, but they also kept him entertained. Elvis, the Colonel, and Vernon Presley never paid the members of the Mafia very much in terms of wages, but Elvis loaned them money for down payments on houses and gave them automobiles, motorcycles, trucks, jewelry, guns, and other expensive gifts. Many of them worked for Elvis more out of friendship than for the money. Some of the men were so close to him that they lived at Graceland from time to time.

Red West joined Elvis on vacation
in Mississippi in the summer of 1956.

IN THE BEGINNING

The germ of the Memphis Mafia began while Elvis toured incessantly in 1955 and 1956. He often asked his cousins Gene and Junior Smith to come with him and his band to help out on the road and to keep him company. When his female fans and their boyfriends began to get unruly, he asked Red West, an all-Memphis football star in high school, to protect them and to do some of the long-distance driving. When West joined the Marines in 1956, he was replaced with Cliff Gleaves and Lamar Fike. After Elvis's mother died in August 1958, several family members and friends visited him for days on end in Texas, where he was stationed in the army. This habit of having a group of friends around continued when he was assigned a tour of duty in Germany. Fike joined him overseas, as did Red West, who had been discharged from the Marines. While in the army, Elvis met a couple of other young men, Charlie Hodge and Joe Esposito, who stayed with him until he died.

TCB

LIKE ANY KING and his court, Elvis and his buddy bodyguards had their own coat of arms. A lightning bolt combined with the initials TCB was designed by Elvis to symbolize the code of honor that he wanted his entourage to live by. TCB stood for "taking care of business," while the lightning bolt represented speed, so the insignia meant "taking care of business in a flash." Elvis wanted everything to be done quickly and efficiently. Elvis had charms made up with this insignia for each member of the Memphis Mafia, and many of the men wore them on chains around their necks.

After Elvis was discharged, he hired Fike, West, Hodge, and Esposito for various jobs ranging from accountant to body-guard, but mostly he hired them for their company.

In 1961, Elvis and his crew went on a brief vacation to Las Vegas. The group wore black mohair suits and sunglasses while they stayed up all night gambling and chasing the Vegas show-girls. Someone around town began calling them Elvis's Memphis Mafia, and the name stuck.

THE MEMPHIS MAFIA

Over the years, the faces in the group changed, but a few men remained with Elvis off and on for much of his career. The most prominent members of the court include Red and Sonny West (who were cousins), Marty Lacker, Joe Esposito, George Klein, Jerry Schilling, Charlie Hodge, Gene Smith, Lamar Fike,

Front from left: George Nichopoulos, Elvis, Red West. Standing from left: Billy Smith, Bill Morris, Lamar Fike, Jerry Schilling, Roy Nixon, Vernon Presley, Charlie Hodge, Sonny West, George Klein, and Marty Lacker.

and Alan Fortas. Some members of the Memphis Mafia didn't work for Elvis exclusively but had their own careers. George Klein worked as a disc jockey in and around Memphis for most of his life. Red West had his Hollywood career as a stuntman and extra, while his cousin Sonny followed him into stunt work. Red also wrote songs for Elvis and other singers, including Ricky Nelson, Pat Boone, and Johnny Rivers.

During the 1960s, members of the Memphis Mafia joined Elvis in Hollywood while he was making movies. At first the group stayed at the Beverly Wilshire Hotel, but eventually Elvis rented a Bel Air mansion that had belonged to the Shah of Iran. The house was the scene of many late-night parties, which often were attended by a host of Hollywood starlets.

Joe Esposito was Elvis's highest-paid employee. He did many things over the years, from bookkeeping to being a bodyguard.

As Elvis grew bored with making movies, his antics and practical jokes got wilder and more elaborate. At first the tedium of movie production was relieved by a football team Elvis organized to pass the time in a constructive manner. Several young actors participated in these games, including Kent McCord, Ty Hardin, Pat Boone, Robert Conrad, Gary Lockwood, and Ricky Nelson. As time went on, Elvis took up more expensive hobbies to fill his time in Hollywood. On one shopping spree while he was making *Tickle Me,* Elvis bought all of his friends motorbikes so they could go riding together.

While on the set in Hollywood, Elvis and his friends pulled practical jokes on members of the cast and crew alike. After Elvis lost respect for his movies, his quest for fun took precedence over his acting. Even pie fights were common. On the

SOUL SEARCHING

THROUGHOUT HIS LIFE, Elvis was extremely interested in spiritual enlightenment, which most members of the Memphis Mafia did not pursue with him. During the 1960s, his interest grew more intense as he realized that he was never going to become a serious actor. Under the influence of a California hairstylist named Larry Geller, Elvis read a great deal about theology, philosophy, and Eastern religions. They pored over books such as *The Impersonal Life* and *Autobiography of a Yogi.* He discussed religion with some of his costars, including Donna Douglas during the production of *Frankie and Johnnie* and Deborah Walley during *Spinout.*

When it seemed to his family and friends that Elvis pushed his pursuit of religious philosophy too far, the Colonel stepped in and stopped it. Geller was then shut out from the group. Obviously, Elvis was looking for meaning in his life, but no one close to him knew how to help him find it. Shoving

Colonel Parker, Elvis, and Larry Geller pose on the set of *Spinout.* Geller was Elvis's hairstylist and part-time spiritual advisor.

Geller aside did little to help Presley's profound disillusionment. Toward the end of Elvis's life, the two renewed their friendship, but by this time Elvis had fallen far from the spiritual path.

set of *Easy Come, Easy Go,* Elvis and director John Rich bickered over the constant mayhem and foolishness that ensued. During one scene, Elvis burst into laughter every time he looked at Red or Sonny West, causing him to blow his lines in take after take. Rich lost his temper and ordered everyone off the set, but Elvis stepped in and set Rich straight. "We're doing these movies because it's supposed to be fun, nothing more," he told his director. "When they cease to be fun, then we'll cease to do them." Later, the group caused so much confusion during the filming of *Clambake* that when production on *Stay Away, Joe* began, a memo came down from the MGM executive offices warning Elvis and the Memphis Mafia about their behavior.

Elvis found working in movies he had little respect for to be tedious, but the downtime in Memphis between films could be worse. One Christmas, Priscilla gave him a slot car system, which inspired him to invest in more cars and track. Plans were made to add a room to Graceland to hold the entire set up, but eventually that hobby was forgotten. For awhile, Elvis and the group amused themselves with a ranch in Mississippi called the Circle G. He bought his whole entourage trucks and horses so that the group could enjoy the ranching life, but they quickly lost interest in that as well. Eventually, he shut down the ranch and sold off its equipment, because it cost too much money to run. In 1969, the Circle G itself was sold. Sometimes Elvis and his buddy bodyguards engaged in "fun" that was actually destructive, such as the time they filled a swimming pool with flashbulbs and shot them to pieces.

Occasionally, the group ventured out into Memphis to seek entertainment. Since Elvis's persistent fans prevented him from going out during normal hours, he rented the Memphian Theater to watch the latest movies as well as older films. Before midnight movies were his passion, Elvis often rented amusement parks or roller-skating rinks after hours for the entertainment of his friends. It was an isolated, insular lifestyle that became more and more removed from the normal world.

PAYING THE PIPER

A cursory glance through the published memoirs of members of the Memphis Mafia reveals that life with Elvis was one of perpetual adolescence. The focus on fun, females, and freedom seemed normal for young men in their early 20s, but there was something irresponsible and rueful about men who pursued this credo when they were pushing 40. During the 1970s,

ELVIS: WHAT HAPPENED? by Red West, Sonny West, and Dave Hebler with Steve Donleavy, 1977

Elvis: Portrait of a Friend by Marty and Patsy Lacker with Leslie E. Smith, 1979

If I Can Dream: Elvis' Own Story by Larry Geller with Joel Spector and Patricia Romanowski, 1980

Me 'N Elvis by Charlie Hodge with Charles Goodman, 1984

Elvis Aaron Presley: Revelations from the Memphis Mafia by Alanna Nash, 1986

Elvis, From Memphis to Hollywood by Alan Fortas with Alanna Nash, 1992

Good Rockin' Tonight by Joe Esposito with Elena Oumano, 1994

Elvis: Still Taking Care of Business by Sonny West with Marshall Terrill, 2007

Elvis called Alan Fortas "Hog Ears." Here Fortas joins Elvis on the set of *It Happened at the World's Fair*.

when Elvis and his crew were either in Las Vegas or on the road, their insular lifestyle grew increasingly self-destructive. There was infighting among the group, and personal relationships with wives and families suffered.

John Lennon once made an insightful statement about Elvis's significance: "Before Elvis, there was nothing." The oft-quoted comment is high praise and a testament to Presley's impact on popular music. But upon Elvis's death Lennon made another statement, which is not as well known but equally as perceptive: "The King is always killed by his courtiers. He is overfed, overindulged, overdrunk to keep him tied to his throne. Most people in the position never wake up."

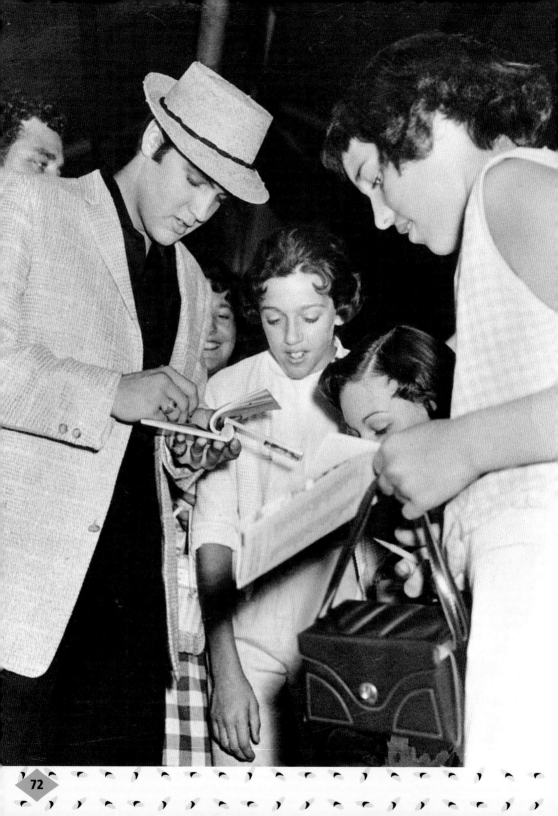

CHAPTER 7

The Wonder of You

Elvis experienced an extraordinary 23-year career in show business. He was an artistic and financial success, and he made an enormous impact on the history of popular music.

SINCE HIS DEATH, Elvis continues to generate revenue for his estate, his popularity among his fans has not diminished, and each new piece of information about his personal life that surfaces serves to keep his name in the news. The word most often associated with this ongoing interest and unwavering support is "phenomenon."

Elvis was always willing to stop and sign autographs for the fans. Because of the sheer number of autographs in existence, they are not worth as much as might be expected.

ELVIS LOVED HIS FANS

Key to the Elvis phenomenon is the loyalty of his fans. Their intense devotion results from a complex combination of circumstances, beginning with Elvis's early career on the country-western circuit. Country-music followers are among the most loyal of popular music fans. Many people who love country music remain devoted to a particular performer for decades, and they often inspire their children to become fans as well.

Elvis signs autographs for fans who were enticed by the Colonel into an "Elvis for President" publicity stunt.

Many of Elvis's most devoted fans became interested in him when he was considered a country singer, and they remained loyal to him even after he became a national rock 'n' roll star.

Elvis, the Colonel, and members of Elvis's family always treated the fans with the utmost consideration from the early days of his success until the very end, when Vernon allowed them to have the flowers from Elvis's funeral. Elvis believed his success was dependent on his fans, and he was always grateful for their loyalty and love. When he was young, he allowed them access to his personal life in a way that no other entertainer would dare. Before Elvis moved to Graceland, fans were always hanging around the Presleys' home. Elvis often invited them onto the patio, and Gladys occasionally served them ice tea. According to Barbara Glidewell, who was befriended by Gladys when a boisterous fan hit Glidewell on the head at one of Elvis's concerts, girls got his phone number and called his house day and night, disrupting the Presley household. The Presleys had their phone number changed several times, but somehow it always slipped out and was circulated among the fans.

AM I THE GIRL FOR ELVIS

N 1958, *Movie Teen Illustrated* asked fans to write in to explain why they should be the girl Elvis marries. The following are actual letters printed in the March 1958 issue.

"I'll do fine for Elvis as a wife because I can't talk very well, but I know how to listen. I also know how to kiss. I've tried it on other boys—just getting in practice. I'm 15, but old for my age.
                —Martha, Chicago, Illinois

"I have a very special reason why I am interested in Elvis. And it is far different from the millions of other girls across the country. But I'll not try voodoo. I have read some girls have.
                —Carol, Decatur, Alabama

"I bake good shoofly pie and cook spareribs and sauerkraut, too. I can play the organ and am learning to play the guitar which means I could play while Elvis sings so he wouldn't get so tired."
                —Mamie, Quakertown, Pennsylvania

Elvis poses with fan Betty Tuttle Goodge, c. 1957. She wrote an Elvis memoir in 1981.

At Graceland, fans often gathered at the gate, and Elvis would walk or ride one of his horses down to sign autographs. When that was not enough for them, fans thought of ingenious ways to get beyond the famous Music Gates. Once, a couple of fans crammed inside a box and mailed themselves to Graceland, where Vernon and his secretaries discovered them. No matter how difficult the fans made Elvis's life by forcing him to live in seclusion, he never complained publicly, and he always had nice things to say about them. In 1957, when the press was abuzz about the way the girls tore his clothes to pieces at every opportunity, he succinctly explained his perspective about the fans to *Illustrated* magazine: "My fans want my shirt. They can have my shirt. They put it on my back."

WHO'S AN ELVIS FAN?

The news media loves to portray Elvis fans as a homogeneous group of middle-aged women who get hysterical at the mere mention of his name or middle-aged men who have never shaved off their muttonchop sideburns. Every August on the anniversary of his death, reporters seek out these stereotypes and trot them in front of the cameras, where they are asked the same tired questions: What is great about Elvis? Why do you think he's still so popular? Is he really dead? The secret that the media doesn't know or doesn't want to uncover is that there is no "typical Elvis fan." Elvis fans represent all ages, all classes, and all walks of life. Despite having never toured outside America and Canada, Elvis attracts fans from all over the world.

Some of his fans are noteworthy or famous in their own right. It should come as no surprise that many pop, rock, and country stars admired Elvis Presley as the performer who established rock 'n' roll as a major force in popular music. From John Lennon to Bob Dylan to Bruce Springsteen, many rock 'n' rollers have publically described Elvis as the "beginning" of it all and, thus, an influence on them. Some African-American singers and musicians, whom Elvis may not have directly influenced, admired him, including James Brown, Jackie Wilson, and Chuck Berry. Such country songwriters as Jerry Reed, Eddie Rabbitt, and Mac Davis, who began their careers in the late 1960s and 1970s, had grown up on Elvis's music and were influenced by it. When Elvis recorded some of their tunes, this influence came full circle.

Musicians and singers are not the only celebrity fans of Elvis; other entertainers and prominent figures also profess to be Presley admirers. Academy Award nominee Eddie Murphy, star of television and films since his years as a cast member on *Saturday Night Live*, was a King-size Elvis fan when he was a teenager. Enamored with Elvis's magnitude as a star, Murphy hoped to attain that level of acclaim for himself. The fact that Elvis conquered more than one arena of entertainment—

recording, live performance, television, and films—also influenced the young comedian, who parlayed his own television stardom into other areas. In addition to television, Murphy has performed standup comedy in clubs, recorded an album, and become a popular film star. When Murphy proclaimed, "Elvis was the greatest entertainer of all time," the focus was on the word "entertainer," alluding to his well-rounded stardom.

Surprisingly, Elvis has attracted a number of fans from the world of politics. In 1970, when Elvis made an impromptu visit to President Richard Nixon in the White House, he was able to stop by and see the President of the United States with very little notice because Nixon aide Bud Krogh was a fan. Twenty-two years later, President Bill Clinton received a boost in his political campaign because he was discovered to be a major Elvis fan, showing that an appreciation for Presley is

Nixon aide Bud Krogh was an Elvis fan, which was instrumental in getting the King in to see the President.

not exclusive to any political party. Clinton's Secret Service code name was Elvis, and the airplane that he often used on his campaign was dubbed *Air Elvis*. His love for Presley and his music was first brought to the attention of the public when he played a heartfelt "Heartbreak Hotel" on the saxophone on *The Arsenio Hall Show*. At the 1992 Democratic National Convention, Senator Al Gore began his acceptance speech for the vice-presidential nomination with the confession that he had "been dreaming of this moment since I was a kid growing up in Tennessee—that one day, I'd have the chance to come here to Madison Square Garden and be the warm-up act for Elvis."

A devotion to Elvis Presley is not exclusive to American politicians. Boris Yeltsin, president of Russia after the fall of Communism, confessed to his obsession with Elvis and his music, "I am a number one fan of Elvis Presley...and, my doctor Tatiana (Uretzkaya) is a fanatic."

In his apartment in Moscow, Yeltsin, who died in 2007, owned a collection of Elvis memorabilia that he began to accumulate at age 27 when he first heard Elvis. "His beautiful voice is from God. But for many years, in our country, it was impossible to get anything from Elvis," recalled Yeltsin. "We had no records or tapes. It was a terrible time for our country, because our government decided for us that Elvis was bad." Yeltsin, who preferred Elvis's slow, sentimental tunes, declared his favorites songs to be "Are You Lonesome Tonight?" and "Welcome to My World."

In the summer of 2006, Japanese Prime Minister Junichiro Koizumi, a lifelong, die-hard fan, arrived in America for an official state visit. After fulfilling his obligations in Washington, D.C., Koizumi flew to Memphis for a personally guided tour of Graceland conducted by Priscilla and Lisa Marie Presley. Throughout his visit, the prime minister could barely contain his enthusiasm and frequently burst into an Elvis song or emulated those famous Presley pelvic gyrations from 50 years earlier.

While Presley's impact on culture often goes unappreciated by a mainstream press still looking for those old stereotypes of the "typical" Elvis fan, the King of Rock 'n' Roll remains one of America's best goodwill ambassadors.

ELVIS WEEK

Each year on the anniversary of Elvis's death, thousands of fans brave the sweltering August heat in Memphis to partake in a week of tributes and memorials that include visiting Graceland, Sun Records, and other Presley haunts. The week culminates on the evening of August 15 with a candlelight ceremony. Early in the evening, fans gather in front of the Music Gates, singing songs and swapping Elvis stories. At 11:00 P.M., two or more Graceland employees walk down to the gate with a torch that has been lit from the eternal flame. As the Music Gates swing open, the fans, each with their own burning candle, climb silently and reverently up the hill behind the house, where they walk single file past the gravesite. The procession can take several hours to pass through Meditation Gardens. It is not only a gesture of respect for Elvis, but it's also proof that Elvis's fans are as faithful after his death as they were during his lifetime. Their devotion reaches beyond the grave.

Elvis Week began unofficially in August 1978, the year after Elvis died. Led by a group called the Texas Country Elvis Presley Fan Club, several fans gathered at the Music Gates and lit candles to pay their respects. The following year, more fan clubs arrived in Memphis to commemorate Elvis on the anniversary of his death. They organized events, though some of the activities overlapped because the clubs did not coordinate with each other. In 1980, Bill Burk of the *Memphis Press-Scimitar,* who later originated *Elvis World,* offered to set up a schedule of the clubs' activities to avoid overlap. This worked until Graceland was opened to the public in 1982, and the estate stepped in to organize events. For about ten years, Elvis Week ran smoothly, with the fan clubs organizing a few events and Graceland arranging a few more.

Fans use newspapers such as the *Elvis Week Event Guide* to navigate Elvis Week.

In the early 1990s, the number of events began to expand, and the pace of Elvis Week accelerated. Currently, the International Tribute Week offers a variety of events and promotes a number of Elvis-related sites over the course of eight days. Though losing some of its informal camaraderie, Elvis Week now offers something for everyone.

Contrary to popular belief, Graceland does not periodically sandblast the wall. The graffiti naturally fades.

THE WRITING ON THE WALL

In the years since Graceland was opened to the public, countless fans have expressed their devotion through an unusual medium—graffiti on the fieldstone wall that borders the property. Fans began writing on the wall while Elvis was still alive, and the groundskeepers did their best to keep it clean. After his death, the task proved too overwhelming, and those who run Graceland decided to leave the heartfelt messages. Today, the wall is essential to the Graceland experience. It not only reveals the many ways that Elvis touched the lives of his fans, but it also serves as a chronicle of major Presley-related revelations.

GRAFFITI

"Elvis , I loved that Jungle Room!"—Jeff

"Elvis—You're all that and a bag of chips."

"You wouldn't have liked the way Caddies look today, anyway."—Mary Lou

"Have a peanut butter sandwich on me, Elvis."—Cheryl

"Dear God: Bolton and Cyrus for Presley?!? Let's Trade!!!"

The joy that comes from experiencing the wall sneaks up on visitors as they begin to read the remarks, declarations, jokes, and endearments. The sheer volume speaks to the continuous stream of fans who come through Graceland, while the many comments written in foreign languages are a reminder that Elvis's popularity is international in scope. On the wall, all comments carry the same weight and all commentators have an equal value. By writing and reading the graffiti, those who experience the wall share a devotion to the musical gifts of the man who rocked their worlds.

Elvis Presley fans have always been intensely devoted, and many have passed that veneration onto other generations as a legacy. Elvis's fans are the most genuine testimony to his talent and his impact on all of us.